LACE BONE BEAST

POEMS & OTHER FAIRYTALES FOR WICKED GIRLS

—

NL SHOMPOLE

LACE BONE BEAST

POEMS & OTHER FAIRYTALES

FOR WICKED GIRLS

COPYRIGHT © 2016 N.L. SHOMPOLE

ISBN-13: 978-1539855866

ISBN-10: 1539855864

forgive
the softness
in your bones

Here is emptiness. Here is a mouth after a recent excavation, black with soot, devoid of kisses. Here are hands, trembling against the soft ache of morning, here are eyes, wet, wide, half-full of sky and loneliness. Here is belly, back, femur, spine, ragged and smooth all at once, all at once. Here are dreams, ink black and speckled, lost behind the eyes. Here is a muted elegy, crow's feet feathered over the eyes like lace. Here are the last strains of a dirge, wild, discordant, free.

THE LACEMAKER

Step from the light
darling,
taste the annihilation, the anarchy,
the abyss.

Come into the dark
darling,
feel the tremors, the ecstasy
the freedom.

THE
WOLF
SAYS
HELLO

Some
lovers
obliterate
you.

THE
WAKING
HOUR

Ghosts
are easy things
to resurrect, and
so are memories,
so are memories.

WHEN THE
NIGHT
GROWS TEETH

I know what it is to fall from the sky, blue feathered, nectar-starved, hurling towards the earth. I know what it is to ache, to want, to miss, to wish for forgetting because anything is easier than remembering. I know what it is to stare at the gathering night, to feel the heartbeat throbbing against the left side of my chest, the thrum-beat-thrum of life, surging, fading. Here, among the shifting seasons and the moving trees I know what if feels like to be amongst the clouds, spine bent, sternum fractured, diaphragm hiccupping as dust devils swallow the sky. I know, I know, I know how it feels to be unmoored, uprooted, pulse churning, driftwood heart caught on the western bank of the Nile, white-knuckle rapids, *drowning*.

Here, here, *here* —so far from home the horizon looks unfamiliar. So far from home the heart stutters out of rhythm.

THE TRAVELER

Hauntings
are not only for the dead,
neither is decay,
neither is despair.

PHANTOMS
& OTHER FAIRYTALES
FOR WICKED
CHILDREN

I

Tell yourself there are no monsters / in the dark /
ignore their rattle / their heart-quake breathing / stare
at the ceiling / until the light comes in / count the
dot-splatter of sun through nail-holes / hide / hide
from the sound of the outside world / shut the self in a
box / darkness is better / no widows / no doors / tell
yourself that the darkness / is better

2

Refuse water / refuse rain / refuse tears / wilt / say
the words out loud / yes / the ones that make your
heart pinch / say them out loud

oblivion.annihilation.desolation.abyss

look it in the eyes / this is how to squeeze the fear /
out of anything / out of everything

3

Dream of chaos / dream / dream of light / of horizons / of poppy fields / of yellow stars / of dandelions / catching fire / on fire / embers descending / a meteorite shower / tremble through the night / at dawn / force knocked knees to stand / shuffle through the dark / till you bump against the spine / the ribcage / till you find the beating heart / follow its rattle to the surface / remember / remember / remember the heart rots / from neglect

see that spark there? that light? it's yours when you're ready

4

Grasp it / hold it / tether yourself to the underside /
of a rising star / pull / heave / excavate the heart / dig
the self out from darkness / from underneath the
cloud / from the dark side of the night / remember /
remember / remember the heart is a tinder-bomb /
half lit / half on fire / half-light / day light / all light
just light

WHEN THE MONSTERS
COME & OTHER FAIRYTALES
FOR WICKED GIRLS

I

Thursday. The sky
is a gray molten
thing.

2

Can't you
smell
how it reeks of
tragedy,
how it reeks of
loss?

SWIMMING
UPRIVER

Oh, darling
loving &
staying isn't
always
the same.

THE
LACEMAKER'S
DAUGHTER

1

I know this much,
if you are not careful
what you love
will cut you,
will break you.

2

I know this much
if you are not careful
you will return
again and again
you will return.

DREAMER
DON'T
DESPAIR

I left my heart in the bottom
of the Danube, whirlwind
echo-chamber, pulsing
wild,
amidst a small flood.

Occasionally, on early mornings
gray-blue raindrops sliding down
the window pane
I hear it,
thump-thump
the heart goes, choked full
of silt
& river water.

WATER SPIRITS
& OTHER THINGS
THAT LURK BENEATH
THE WAVES

In the event of a cataclysm

Fall, fall out of the sky with all the force of a burning plane, swallow a kaleidoscope of butterflies if only to feel the softness of their wings between your teeth. Cry, let the saltwater burn the open wounds, crumble, disintegrate into ash and bone and dust, let the winds carry you out to sea.

DISASTERS
OF THE HEART
& OTHER
CATACLYSMS

Abracadabra
he says
&
my heart sparks
a full-bodied
nebula
onto the
kitchen floor.

THE MAGICIAN

lace/bone/beast
  when night comes
   roaring in.

   slow/steady/brave
    when disaster knocks
     you right off your feet.

    breathe/breathe/breathe
    when the dark comes
   with sharpened teeth.

   breathe / breathe / breathe
  for here comes the dawn,
here comes the dawn.

      SLOW / STEADY / BRAVE
      & OTHER MANTRA'S
      FOR LONELY GIRLS

There will be blood
there will be tears
there will be despair
there will be days so dark
they bleed into night
each undistinguishable
from the other.

There will be storms
there will be ruin
there will be wreckage
there will be fire
that will raze everything
down to bone, down to ember,
down to ash.

& if you want it
there will be hope
bright and ravenous
but only if you want it,
only if you want it.

NO ONE IS COMING
TO SAVE YOU & OTHER FAIRYTALES
FOR WICKED GIRLS

Remember,
the heart rots
from neglect.

MEDITATIONS
FOR THE LONELY
HEART

1

They will tell you
about the night
but no one warns you
how dark it gets.

2

No one tells you
how the melancholy
seeps in, halfway through
the morning, steeped
in indigo clouds,
and the remnants
of last night's dream.

QUARTER PENCE
FOR THE MIDNIGHT
TRAIN

There will be days that feel blue, heavy, numb. You wake up and everything feels out of touch, the sour taste of a bad dream still in your mouth. It will seem as if the world is burning down around you, and the smoke is so thick it burns your eyes and clogs your throat and all you can do is huddle in bed and counting your heart beats. I won't lie to you. There will be days when it seems like the world is breaking apart around you despite everything, in spite of everything. It isn't, not yet, not yet.

MONSTERS
DON'T LIVE IN CAVES
& OTHER FAIRYTALES
FOR WICKED CHILDREN

Don't you see
how weathered
I am,
how tired
I am
of begging?

SALT
& SHADOWS

Decades between
you and I
have not softened
the longing.

HOMECOMING

Truth
last night
I was Shiva,
backbone bent thrice,
third eye full of stars.

Truth,
I am the battlefield
where gods go to war.

Truth,
hyperion came home to die
between my thighs.

Truth
There is no fear
beneath my ribcage.

Truth,
I can make you beg,
I can make you beg.

THE
REVIVER'S
LOVER

Rain, dissolve like a river bank at the height of flood-season, dig out all the roots that tether you to the shore, cut through silt, through sand, through rock if only to remind yourself of the way back home.

Burn, spark like a wildfire at the height of fire-season, devour the shrub, the trees, the forest. Devour the wilderness and leave a trail of ash like breadcrumbs through the woods if only to remind yourself of the way back home.

THEY
CALLED
ME
WICKED

Some days I forget myself, I sit by the window at the
corner café, hot tea sloshing in my cup
              & disappear between drops of rain.

Some days I step into a field of ruins older than time,
              & somewhere the tender-thick strains
              of a concerto filter through, coloring
              the sky.

Some days hope rattles in my chest, echoing so deep &
sharp in the hollow beneath my ribs that my
diaphragm aches
              & I cannot help but think there must
              be an art to finding bones in the ashes.

MELANCHOLIA

/ silence steals the heart
    / silence stills the heart
        / silence, still is the heart.

MEDITATIONS
FOR THE LOST

Last night
last night
last night
I dreamt
of you.

&

THERE
YOU
WERE

November comes
with the suddenness
of yellow leaves
thick with morning
frost.
An entire year *autumn-ing*
between breaths.

December finds me
mid-metamorphosis.
A lamb,
ribcage & full-wool gusset
to hold in the blood, to hold in
the beating heart.

January dawns,
stalactites & ice white skies.
The bone-cold chill of dusk
turns me
wolf.
Bloody mouthed,
hungry.

LAMB FOR SLAUGHTER
& OTHER FAIRYTALES
FOR WICKED GIRLS

Hold me
against the
sharpness
of your
teeth.

TO THE
WOLF
I
SAY

There are no potions for un-remembering a name, for dispelling pain, how it claws its way beneath your skin, shaking through your bones, devouring, *devouring*.

There are no spells for erasing darkness as it gnaws a hole in the soft underside of your belly, sharpening teeth against flesh, against bone, against will.

ARE YOU SHEEP,
OR WOLF?
& OTHER FAIRYTALES
FOR WICKED
CHILDREN

Here we are

the sky a mournful blue / my heart / half-stuck
unraveling / your eyes pitch black
full / so full
of want

Here we are

pulse like the ninth wave / of a tsunami / caught
between the ribcage & the sternum
caught between / oblivion
& surrender

THE
MAGICIAN'S
LOVER

1

Once,
October sky rust red
& fading,
I dreamt I was a
silk-worm, belly stretched
full of silk, slowly
weaving my burial
shroud.

2

Once,
October hungry
& full of teeth
I dreamt of growing wings
every shade of night,
I woke up ravenous
& demolished
the moon.

THERE ONCE
WAS A
MAGICIAN

Fall,
fall out of the sky
with all the grace
of a crashing plane.

SONG FOR THE
BROKEN-HEARTED

Love,
soften
the
rebellion
in my
bones.

CONVERSATIONS
WITH THE
REVIVER

One day everything you've ever known will splinter, a tree caught on the wrong side of a storm, uprooted.

He will come home at lunchtime, pull you out of a painting to tell you that he's leaving, that there is nothing left for him in you and you'll swear your heart has turned to stone, to ice, to marble at the heart of Rome.

꙳

the darkness will threaten to drown you,

꙳

the darkness will threaten to devour you whole

One day you will wake up and everything you have ever known will fragment and light will filter in through the sky like lightning out of season and the numbness will wash away, will wash away.

CAUGHT DOWNRIVER
DURING
FLOOD SEASON

Darling, here is a secret
there is nothing beautiful
about disaster, about breaking,
there is nothing beautiful
about bones dislocating,
crumbling to ash,
crumbling to salt.

I will tell you again,
and again, and again
there is nothing
beautiful about despair,
about the shadows that come
on raiding winds, about the wreckage
they leave behind, the wreckage,
the wreckage, the wreckage.

Darling, here is a secret,
beauty comes after the disaster,
after the haunting, after the
hours spent lost among the salvage,
beauty comes in the midst
of survival, of reconstruction,
of revival.

CHOOSE THE DAWN

Truth,
I am all teeth.

HOW TO TURN
WOLF,
A MANUAL

The softness in your bones is
not / has not / will never be weakness

The tears that burn to the surface
in the face of grief or affront are not / will never be
signs of a faint heart

It's only right that some days you will be more
storm than sky
more rage than softness
more fury than forgiveness

&
That's alright,
that is alright

FORGIVE
THE SOFTNESS
IN YOUR BONES

Hold steady when disaster comes. Turn rock, turn rain, turn water —timber house splintered, fallen. Turn broken bones, faint-heart, a bag of grief and melancholy. Turn farmer waiting for harvest, waiting for the evening sun. Turn shepherd, turn sheep lost among the cliffs. Yearn for home when evening comes. Weep when the dark wipes out the sky. Turn glass figurine sitting in a windowpane. Turn everything you thought you remembered. Turn everything you thought you knew.

—

Turn everything you thought you knew. Turn everything you thought you remembered. Turn glass figurine sitting in a windowpane. Weep when the dark wipes out the sky, yearn for home when evening comes. Turn sheep lost among the cliffs, turn shepherd waiting for evening sun, waiting for harvest. Turn farmer, faint-heart, a bag of grief and melancholy. Turn broken bones —timber house splintered, fallen. Turn rain, turn water, turn rock. Hold steady when disaster comes.

METAMORPHOSIS,
A MANUAL

Love,
if nothing else,
forgive yourself.

MANTRA'S &
MEDITATIONS FOR
THE LOST

I

March me, blue-feathered and nectar-drunk towards the edge of the sky. Cast a net on a willow tree, arrest me from flight, watch me turn into a comet as I fall through the clouds.

You say you rescued me, and I believe you, *I believe you*. But sometimes a memory unearths itself from my femur and I remember the taste of air and rainy seasons.

Feed me, birdwatcher feed me. Fill me up with nectar, with strange language and honey that tastes of foreign things, summer things, of things in the dark that bite just as hard, just as deep.

2

Weep, birdwatcher weep but let me go. Let me go before the breaking, before my feathers molt, before the tongue turns on itself, half-starved and bluing.

Love me but set me free. Set me free before I turn caterpillar, before I turn silk-worm, before hibernation quakes through my bones and the metamorphosis eviscerates everything that I am, everything that I have ever been.

Listen, birdwatcher, listen to the hymn of the hummingbird's wingbeat against all that yellow sky, listen to the heartbeat before torpor sets in, before the cicada wakes from winters grip.

THE BIRDWATCHER'S WIFE
& OTHER FAIRYTALES
FOR WICKED GIRLS

Devour me,
but leave the bones,
shuck the flesh away with twine
or the edge of an oyster knife
hook under the elbows
into the tender of the socket
count the ribs
& the knobbed range of the spine
thread the hair till it's loose
make blankets or ink
& with all that's left
string it through
the hollow
where the heart beats
& beats & beats
a faint staccato
remembering home
devour me, I say,
devour me
but leave the bones.

TO THE NIGHT
I SAY—
& OTHER FAIRYTALES
FOR WICKED
CHILDREN

Sunday,
he makes you
breakfast

& all you can think
is how much
you hate
the smell of eggs
first thing in the
morning.

**THE
LOVER & THE
TRANSLATOR**

There is a flood
somewhere inside me / dreams the shape of
Venice / abandoned / an entire city / waterlogged

& drowning beneath my skin.

There is a graveyard
somewhere inside me / incense rising from the
diaphragm / Venice on fire / burning

the softest hiccup turning it all to ash.

There is a shipwreck
somewhere inside me / rotting bones bend / fold
crumble / the water / all the water / surges with the
night tide

& threatens to overwhelm.

A DIARY OF
LOST THINGS

There is no
graveyard
more haunting
than a former
lover's eyes.

SMALL TRUTHS
& OTHER THINGS
NO ONE TELLS YOU

ARE YOU AWARE
OF HOW CLOSELY YOU RESEMBLE
THE NIGHT SKY, IN ALL ITS DARK,
STRANGE, JAGGED BEAUTY.

ARE YOU AWARE
OF HOW CLOSELY YOU RESEMBLE
A GALAXY, MID-ANNIHILATION?

DISINTEGRATING
INTO NOTHING
BUT LIGHT
—BRIGHT, CAPTURED
AGAINST A NEAR-BLACK
SKY.

THEY WILL CALL
YOU WICKED

LOVE THE BODY THROUGH
ALL THE STAGES OF RUIN, AND
RESURRECTION.

LOVE THE BODY THROUGH
THE DARK OF WINTER, AND
INTO SPRING.

LOVE THE BODY
FOR IT HAS HOUSED YOU
THROUGH THE COLLAPSE, AND
THE CATASTROPHE.

THE HEART
IS A CASKET
FOR FORGOTTEN
THINGS

IT SEEMS UNLIKELY, NOW, TETHERED AS YOU ARE TO THE DYING THROES OF RUIN, BUT THIS IS HOW YOU WILL BE BIRTHED, FROM THE BONES, FROM THE WRECKAGE, FROM THE AFTERMATH OF THE STORM.

AFTER THE COLLAPSE

TRUTH,
I AM A MUSEUM
OF RUIN
&
RESURRECTION.

THE REVIVER

Teeth don't
grow in the dark.

HOW TO BE
THE BEAST
& OTHER FAIRYTALES
FOR WICKED
GIRLS

I

The night has become too dark for sleep, so I wait for the pink light of dawn to filter in through half-open curtains, before sleep overtakes me.

I dream in bouts of sweat and fury, wake up tangled in twisted sheets, sunlight burning through the room, bones trembling from another nightmare.

I dream, I dream, I dream,
 I made a bargain with the devil,
his heart for mine,
then he devoured it whole.

2

The bed is sinking, folding under like the sea after a shipwreck, turbulent. In the moment before drowning clothes become fishing nets, dragging me down below the water, below the waves.

I can't breathe, I can't breathe,
I can't breathe so I strip down to skin
I strip down to bone
curl up on the couch and wait
for morning to come.

3

I count the fan's blades as they whir through the heat,
I count breaths until the fear leaves, until I feel brave
enough to let the sleep pull me in deep.

*I dream
of growing teeth
and blue feathered wings
of being brave, brave
brave.*

Brave enough, brave enough, brave enough to take
flight, brave enough to fall.

I DREAM
OF LIGHT

1

Last night
my bones rattled
& whistled
to the call of the
samovar.

2

At dawn
steam,
lace-boned & fragile
boils over.

3

I
evaporate.

THE DREAMER

There is no
revolution
like the revolution
of a heart
for itself.

REVOLUTION,
A MANUAL FOR THE
SOFT-HEARTED

I

This is how to dismantle a life, us sitting at the dinner table, last night's supper (untouched) still between us, the sweet sour perfume of rancid rice and half drank wine telling us it's long past time to walk away.

2

This is how to untangle a life, how to unravel the bitter sweet constellation fading between us. This is how to cover the ruins, mourn for the dead, the dying, the decaying remnants of a dream. This is how to bury the loss. The fighting, the late nights driving through the city because the house is too big without you, too empty, and somehow too full of thoughts of you... too full of tears, and hope, always hope.

3

This is how to un-remember, this is how to keep the ghosts at bay —walk away and don't look back. Not until the memories have been reduced to ash, to dust. When the sadness comes creeping in, and it will, *it will, it will*, take a bath. Wash the blue tint of phantoms from your skin and choose the dawn, no matter what, choose the dawn.

DIRGE
FOR THE
DREAMER

Chew October up and spit out the rusted nails, bend the seasons to your beck and call, snuff out September then spend the morning writing a eulogy. Break November in half, bury its pieces out back and demand the noon-day sun with all the heat of a volcano back into the sky. Wrestle December from winter's grip and wear the frost like a royal cloak. Wave your hand and watch all the willows bow, branches scraping first snow of the ground. Sing deep in the night and listen to the wolves return your howl, listen to the wolves return your howl.

HERE COMES
THE WILDELING WITCH
& OTHER FAIRYTALES
FOR GOOD GIRLS

Once upon a time,
Icarus with wings of
feathers and wax
soared, and touched the sky.

Once upon a time
Icarus , caught on fire,
mid-flight, and plummeted
towards the sea.

Once upon a time
Icarus, wax melted
and featherless
sank beneath the waves
and drowned.

2

Refuse the drowning, refuse the pull of salt water on your skin, refuse the tide, refuse the storm. Write yourself into existence because no one else will.

THE
HISTORIAN

I

Take apart the story, pour your truth inside it until it sparks and catches fire, until the sun eats up the sky and all that's left is the memory of warmth.

2

Truth,
I was Icarus
once, drowning
beneath the waves.

Truth,
I was Icarus
once, soaring
above the clouds.

THE
HISTORIAN'S
LOVER

I

October is dead and buried when the prospector
arrives, briefcase in hand and a wolf-teeth smile.

'I smelt water, down around
the bend.'
He says.
'Came all this way just to see.'

2

Coal black eyes piercing flesh, through skin, through bone. Draws a map, marks the spot with a dot-red pin right over the pulse.

'A well like this will never run dry,' He says hungrily, 'Never!'

'Just a bit further' He murmurs, tongue pressed against teeth, ice cold fingers and a pick axe half an inch from the heart.

'Never!'
He says,
'A heart like this will never empty.'

Years will pass before you look back, before you stop running from the place that broke you. Days will slip into months of fog, months of drowning the remembrance of a war that still bites through your skin at night, slowly, softly.

Somehow, you'll find yourself standing on the threshold overlooking a graveyard of forgotten things, memories thick with ash will overtake you and your hands will shake and your spine will threaten to fold like a paper sculpture in the rain.

Hours will stretch to the sound of your heartbeat and panic, longer still before you forget the taste of fear and loneliness souring the back of your throat.

So bury the thing that haunts you, that pulls you back and remember that the carnage can't get to you, not anymore, not anymore. Remember the spirit once halved, can stitch itself back together.

NIGHT
COMES
ROARING
IN

I

Are you there
love?
I remember you,
eyes half-sun,
half naked sky
half-moon.

2

Are you there
love?
I remember you
skin like fire dappled
obsidian, ink black
lovely
a small infinity
looking back at me.

A SONG FOR
THE LOVERS

Truth
my ribcage
is the softest part
of me.

MEDITATIONS

Cry, cry black feathers down you back, demolish the moon and spit back a mouthful of blood and entrails when they come asking for your sons. Cry disaster, cry calamity, cry a mourning song in octaves only the dogs can hear. Cry a long dead river back into being, cry fire, cry panic, cry light burning through coal-black-skin and demand the dawn, demand the dawn with all its hope and none of its rain. Cry, cry the molasses back into the body, cry the stutter back into the heartbeat, cry, cry the blackbirds back into flight, cry the blackbirds back into the morning sky.

FUNERAL
FOR
CROWS

Remember,
we don't stop loving
the ones who
betray us.

MEDITATIONS &
SMALL TRUTHS FOR THE
BROKEN HEARTED

Daylight is fading. We are on a blanket on the lawn, indigo light washing over us when you ask me —*what I know of sorrow?* I run my tongue across my teeth and think for a minute, then a minute more before I turn to you. The obsidian in your eyes threatens to drown me so I look away.

What can I say? I have no words for the darkening thing in my belly. I can't find a way to tell you how sorrow stretches itself into a wide, edge-less ache. How it resembles the glass smooth surface of a long forgotten lake, endless and deep as the horizon. How it rattles and coils slowly in the gut like a sea monster, hungry, always hungry.

Somewhere in the coming dark a cricket chirps, shattering this thing between us. I have no words answer you with, so we sit, fingertips grazing, stars combusting against the gathering night.

LOVE
TELL ME
YOUR DREAMS

May I tell you about shedding skin? About burrowing so deep inside the sky, inside the country, inside the town, inside the life, inside foreign things and foreign people and foreign accents. Accents so smooth they almost, *almost* drown out the smell of home.

May I tell you about the rediscovery? About the shaking loose from bedrock, to find the bones still calling for milk, for blood, for the scent of smoke and mud and home buried so deep beneath the memory it takes years to unearth.

May I tell you about the return? About the thickening of the tongue, the mouth, the language, the stories, the echo of songs in the blood until there's nothing left but home, rattling deep within the bones.

I USE ONE
LANGUAGE
TO DEVOUR
THE OTHER

1

Darling,
I have grown
accustomed
to the falling sky,
to the way loneliness,
gathers like mist
falling over dawn.

2

Darling,
I have grown
accustomed
to getting lost,
to wandering so far from home
the sky no longer resembles
anything I know.

3

Darling
I have grown
accustomed
to breaking, collapsing,
to the sharp edge of the night
against my skin,
to the soft edge
of disaster
at the break of day.

LACE
BONE
BEAST

I am inhabited / by silence / the sound of night seeping in /   falling in / water rushing over stone / crickets before the dawn / creeps in / dense as a cedar forest / catching fire

I am ravaged / by existence / weathered / wind beaten / rain soaked / into living

IN THE
AGE
OF
MAMMOTHS

I

Dream, dream, dream all the dreams. Be all the monsters, hungry, ravenous for heartbeats, for light. Be the sun, a sudden storm, explode on a cold November day, swallow the ocean, swallow the earth, gather the dark around you, be the night and wipe out the sky.

Devour the world then spit out all the bones. Pick your teeth with hummingbird feathers, hum the tune your lover sang before he broke you in half the same way continents shift away from each other, slowly, then all at once, all at once.

2

Sing, sing all the songs. Feel the echo of a thunderstorm shaking in your bones, loud, loud, loud as a wild-bird chorus in May. Blink, watch the world vanish before your eyes, blink, watch the world reappear the way you want it, steel and lace.

3

Rage, rage with all the fury of a typhoon, a hurricane ripping up the coastline out of season. Rage like a tornado devouring a field of flowers, scatter all the petals like snowflakes mid-blizzard because there is nothing soft about you, because there is everything soft about you.

4

Unravel, unravel like a spool of lace in your grandmother's attic, crumble to dust at the slightest touch. Shiver, shake, tremble, spark. Spark like lightning on a clear day, sudden, brilliant, blinding.

—

When you are done, drape yourself over everything lovely and wonder at all the beauty in your bones, all the softness of your ribcage. Wonder at the way the light reflects off the obsidian in your eyes an hour before sunset, wonder at the way his eyes light up when he sees you.

5

Be all of it, a dichotomy, raining and sunning all at once. A hyena's wedding mid-march, a conundrum of tears and laughter in April. Be, be all of it, warrior with a wildflower heart and a spine like steel, sharpen your teeth but don't forget the dreamer just because the world called you to war. Dream, dream, dream all the dreams.

LIGHTNING,
WILDFLOWERS
& OTHER FAIRYTALES
FOR WICKED
GIRLS

Remember,
breaking is not the same
as dying.

MEDITATIONS
FOR THE
SOFT-HEARTED

He will offer
you the world,
your palms will sweat
your legs will shake
you will be afraid
you will look him in the eyes
and say yes anyway.

WISE GIRL
DON'T BE AFRAID
OF FALLING

Burn,
darling, hot
as a lightning bolt,
bright
as a collapsing star.

NOTHING
COMES
FROM
NOTHING

When you are offered magic, take it. When you are offered joy, curl your fingers around it, revel in it. Drink, until your stomach is stretched full against the jagged edge of your ribcage. When you are offered love, accept it. Even if it is only for a day, an hour, even if it's only for a second.

MEDITATIONS & OTHER
MANTRAS FOR THE
SOFT-HEARTED

I promise
        there's more softness
               in me.

ELEGY

February, spin shadows out of fog. Spin phantoms early morning, blue and drowning. Spin cottonwood skin mid-May, begging for sun, begging for sky. Dream a sweltering dream in August, house walls sweating at midnight, rust and morning-dew in October. Dusk, November, spark firewood. Spark embers like fireflies, waltzing to the fading light. Slow and steady and brave. When nighttime comes, spark a fire in his obsidian eyes and unravel, and unravel.

THE
LACEMAKER'S
LOVER

I

Here is the thing about being stranded at sea, everything is a metaphor, waves for the sadness, clouds for the despair, the heart an island jutting out of the sea, a lonely, forlorn thing.

2

Here is the thing about being caught on the underside of a wave, lost in the wilderness of a sea that stretches from horizon to horizon. Water rises and churns beneath the surface in the wake of a hurricane, a sea storm can rise of out nothing high enough to break ships, bring titans down.

3

Here is the thing about learning how to breathe under water, sometimes you swallow a lung full of salt that burns all the way down. No one will tell you this, but drowning isn't gentle, not even for fish, not even for those birthed at sea.

4

Here is what no one will tell you. Living is a lot like being shipwrecked months away from shore. Nothing but black sky and blue water everywhere you look. Sometimes, sometimes you'll hear sea creatures whisper. Sometimes you'll dream you have gills or fins, or eight hearts, all of them yearning for the shore.

—

But dreams are merely dreams and the tide will come roaring in and the fisherman will loosen his grasp and the silver netting meant to save you will slip away. Because, because the truth is no one can save you but you, because the truth is we either survive the catastrophe or we drown.

5

So take a deep breath love, because all disasters come unseen. One day the ship will go under and the lifeboats will catch fire and you'll have no choice but to swim.

When it ruin comes, and it will, *it will, it will,* do your best to avoid the vortex above the wreckage. Swim, paddle like hell for open water, keep your head above the waves even when your lips turn blue, and the cold turns your blood to ice. Even when you've forgotten what it is like to have legs, or how it feels to stand on solid ground, or how it feels to have a spine of steel and lungs devoid of water.

Swim!
Keep your head above the water, above the waves. Swim, no matter what, *no matter what.*

HOW TO SURVIVE
A SHIPWRECK & OTHER
FAIRYTALES FOR
WICKED GIRLS

Once,
I went three weeks
in absolute silence.

I blink-drowned
& vanished.

MEDITATIONS

There is no collapse here, no wreckage, no church on fire, no ash, no peonies rotting in flooded fields, no tears that taste like salt and copper, no salt, no copper, no emergency ice-cream bought with pennies, no ceramic shards that smell like copper, no gutted piggybank hurling off the shelf —stunned senseless. There is no sight to see, no roadside wreckage on Monday morning. Only a heart —broken, already stitching itself back together.

HEALING TAKES TIME
& OTHER FAIRYTALES FOR
WICKED GIRLS

I

It's an hour before dusk,

&
debris is burning up the sky,
&
shards of light devour the clouds,
devour the crows
&
all the fireflies
&
meteorites freeze
in ecstasy
a moment before
collision.

2

Small cracks fracture the night sky,

> it is 3 a.m. when all your
> heartbeats tumble out,
> &
> dissipate.

A GUIDE
TO FALLING
IN LOVE

Remember,
everything that matters
comes slowly, the teeth
the bravery, the strength
the softness.

MEDITATIONS
FOR THE
SOFT-HEARTED

also by n.l. shompole

poetry

Cassiopeia at midnight
Anatomy of Surrender
Heaven Water Blood
Phantoms as Euphemisms for Disaster
       [Spectre Specter Blue Ravine]

upcoming works

Zamora
Republic of Two Moons

Shompole's work is now available on Amazon.com or
directly through her website
+ Kingdomsinthewild.com/store

author

N.L Shompole is a writer, artist and poet. She was born in Kenya where she spent her childhood. She lives, studies & creates in the San Francisco Bay Area and is currently working on a several projects including the upcoming novella Republic of Two Moons.

She can be found on

Website / Kingdomsinthewild.com
Instagram / @NLShompole
Goodreads.com/NLShompole

CPSIA information can be obtained
at www.ICGtesting.com
Printed in the USA
BVOW03s0125110817
491811BV00001B/17/P